THE ESSENTIAL ™

John James Audubon

BY ANNETTE BLAUGRUND

THE WONDERLAND
PRESS

Harry N. Abrams, Inc., Publishers

THE WONDERLAND PRESS

The Essential™ is a trademark
of The Wonderland Press, New York
The Essential™ series has been created by The Wonderland Press

Series Producer: John Campbell
Series Editor: Julia Moore
Project Manager: Adrienne Moucheraud
Series Design: The Wonderland Press

Library of Congress Catalog Card Number: 99-73513
ISBN 0-7407-0291-2 (Andrews McMeel)
ISBN 0-8109-5807-4 (Harry N. Abrams, Inc.)

Portions of the text have been drawn from *John James Audubon:
The Watercolors for The Birds of America* (Villard, 1993),
by Annette Blaugrund and Theodore E. Stebbins, Jr.

Distributed by Andrews McMeel Publishing
Kansas City, Missouri 64111-7701

Printed in Hong Kong

Harry N. Abrams, Inc.
100 Fifth Avenue
New York, NY 10011
www.abramsbooks.com

Contents

Artist, Romantic, Spinmeister Extraordinaire

Filmmaker Alfred Hitchcock was not the only one with a thing for the birds. The saga of **John James Audubon** (1785–1851)—at once a tale of romance, idealism, hardship, and magnificent artwork—is an astounding example of talent and ambition, even by today's go-go standards.

Coming of age just as amateur scientists were starting to attentively document the natural world, Audubon combined science and art into the legendary illustrations featured in *The Birds of America* (1827–39) and in the less well known *The Viviparous Quadrupeds of North America* (1845–48). To this day, his work retains its hold on the public's imagination, for reasons we'll explore here. Fantastic stories about his life persist—that he was the long-lost son of King Louis XVI of France, that he was a student of legendary French painter **Jacques-Louis David** (1748–1825), that he hunted with American pioneer **Daniel Boone** (1734–1820). Don't laugh, but it was Audubon himself who both invented and perpetuated these myths—a PR maven who manipulated his persona to conform with 19th-century romantic ideas. He appeared to the French and the English as an all-American frontiersman, decked out in buckskin and telling outrageous tales of adventure. Not only did the foreign nobles enjoy his flamboyance, but they subscribed to his *Birds* series with great enthusiasm.

Home of John James Audubon's father, Couëron France

Confused Origins

John James Audubon's unique achievements were the result of unwavering energy, tenacity, a sense of romance and adventure—and great natural talent. His prosperous father, French sea captain **Jean Audubon** (1744–1818), had purchased a sugar plantation in Sainte-Domingue, West Indies (now Haiti), during an interval between France's wars with the dreaded British. While there, he installed French chambermaid **Jeanne Rabine** (1758–1785) as mistress of the plantation and, with her, produced a young bastard son, **Jean**, who was born on April 26, 1785. His mother died when the future illustrator was less than one year old.

At the age of three, Jean was sent across the Atlantic to his father's home in Couëron, France, to be raised by Captain Audubon's lawfully wedded (and rich) wife, **Anne Moynet** (c. 1730–1821), otherwise known as Madame Aubudon. In these important formative years, the toddler faced the loss of his mother, an abrupt change in surroundings, and life with a "new" family in a foreign country.

FYI: **His name**—During the Reign of Terror in France (1794), the Catholic Church was outlawed and so were Christian names. **Jean Rabine** was called by the made-up name **Fougère**, or fern. When he was legally adopted by his father and stepmother in 1794, he became **Jean-Jacques Audubon**. He later anglicized his name to **John James Audubon** when he established himself in the United States. In his time, he was considered a Creole, which meant a person of European descent born in the West Indies or elsewhere among the early French, Portuguese, or Spanish settlements of North America.

While it's always iffy to speculate, these circumstances no doubt profoundly influenced the future artist's personality and his sense of belonging. From an early age, Audubon felt great shame at being illegitimate. His compulsion to succeed, his endurance against hardship, his theatrical inventions, and his perseverance at all cost were motivated, at least in part, by these early years.

A Childhood in Brittany

Young Jean's talents and natural curiosity were fostered by his upbringing in France, which included a gentleman's education: the classics, drawing, violin, fencing, and dancing. When Jean was 11, his father enrolled him in the naval academy at Rochefort-sur-Mer, where he spent three years proving to his father that he was not cut out for a life at sea.

From early childhood, Jean seems to have been obsessed with documenting and studying wildlife—animals as well as birds—which at first he rendered in pastel and graphite on paper. Whenever possible, he escaped into the woods to observe nature, collect specimens, and draw. It is likely that Audubon learned to use pastels either at the Free Academy of Drawing in Nantes or through manuals tailored to amateurs.

FYI: **Pastels and graphite**—Pastel is ground color, gum, and water compounded into a crayon. Graphite is lead, similar to that used in pencils. Pastel was very popular in 18th-century France as a medium for both professional and amateur artists. Prominent pastelists of the period,

Maurice Quentin de La Tour (1704–1788), **Jean-Baptiste Perronneau** (1715–1783), and **Jean-Baptiste Chardin** (1699–1779), revealed the exquisite possibilities of the medium in the hands of professionals. Nevertheless, works in pastels and in watercolors were eventually stigmatized, as these mediums were considered suitable only for women hobbyists.

Whatever experiences inspired the young artist, he soon developed a unique perspective. While his claims that he had studied with Jacques-Louis David cannot be substantiated, he was influenced by the prevalent Neoclassical style of clear outlines and geometric compositional framework inspired by David.

Given David's importance and popularity in France during Audubon's formative years, it's no wonder that the young naturalist chose to associate himself with the famous artist.

Coming to America

Jean emigrated to the United States in 1803 at the age of 18 in order to escape being drafted into Napoleon's army. Though he anglicized his name to John James Audubon, he would never lose his memorable French accent. In 1812, he became a U.S. citizen.

In America, Audubon's first assignment was to manage a modest farm that his father had purchased several years earlier, just outside Philadelphia. There, he lived the life of a country gentleman, drawing birds for his own enjoyment, and paying little attention to the management of the property, which was already well run by a business manager and a farmer who worked the land. Audubon loved the wide-open lands and dense forests of his new home, and it wasn't long before he set out on expeditions to explore the terrain, listen to the wondrous sounds of birds unfamiliar to him, and take up his passion for drawing. These early sketches would prove to be the groundwork for a career that would last several more decades and would culminate in the spectacular artwork that brings people joy to this day.

He was a mass of contradictions, in part because of his troubled past, but these were contradictions completely true to his time. Popular in Mill Grove, Pennsylvania, as a *bon vivant* ("not a ball, a skating match

OPPOSITE
Detail from
Magnolia Warbler
1829

or a house- or riding party took place without me," he once said), he was also an excellent hunter and marksman. One day, he and a friend were out ice skating, and the friend threw his cap into the air as a challenge. Audubon—not slowing one bit—aimed, fired, and bullseyed the target.

Off to the Woods

Whenever the young artist went out into the woods, he carried with him a gun, a sketchpad, pencils, and his ornithology reference books, which soon enough he found inaccurate and lacking in information. (*Ornithology* is the study of birds.) Like many of the amateur naturalists of his day, Audubon ended up having to teach himself. He collected a treasure trove of birds' nests and eggs (their insides blown out through needle holes), along with stuffed raccoons, squirrels, opossums, snakes, lizards, and dried frogs.

In trying to understand more about the lives of birds, he was one of the first to use *banding* to identify some individual phoebies (i.e., tying silver strings to the legs of some young birds to see if they would return the following year to their Pennsylvania nests). He would sit for hours studying a particular bird's behavior, one day even tracking a Snowy Owl to its hunt-

ABOVE
Mill Grove (the estate today is an Audubon museum)

OPPOSITE
Thomas Birch
Mill Grove Farm
Perkioman Creek
Pennsylvania
Oil on wood. c. 1820s
16 1/4 x 24 1/4"
(36.56 x 54.56 cm)

John James
Audubon
c. 1810
Engraving

ing site, where it lay flat down on the ice of a frozen river, recalling later that it lay "with its head down near the water…. One might have supposed the bird sound asleep. The instant a fish rose to the surface, the owl thrust out the claw that was next to the water and drew it out like lightning."

Jean's early drawings—such as the *Belted Kingfisher* of July 15, 1808—reveal static profile images that are, however, precisely observed and accurately rendered. Some, like the *Long-Tailed Mountain Titmouse*, dated January 22, 1805, were amateurish, patterned after the prized illustrations he had seen in *Histoire naturelle, générale et particulière* by Georges Louis LeClerc, the **Comte de Buffon** (1707–1788).

He may also have been influenced by the work of the court painter to Louis XV, **Jean-Baptiste Oudry** (1686–1755), whose hunting scenes of animals and still lifes with game decorated royal palaces and châteaux, as well as Sèvres porcelain and Gobelins and Beauvais tapestries and upholstery.

*Long-Tailed
Mountain
Titmouse*
1805
Pastel and
graphite on
paper
12 x 9 ³/₈"
(27 x 21.26 cm)

Nᵒ 5.   La Mésange a longue queue — de Buffon.   Oriziale peut nantz
         the Long Tailed Mountain tit-mouse.   le queue de poilée
Le 22 Janvier 1805.

Black-billed Cuckoo. Male 1. F.2
COCCYZUS ERYTHROPHTHALMUS.
Plant. Magnolia grandiflora.

Engraved, Printed, & Coloured by R. Havell & Son, London. 1876.

Black-Billed Cuckoo. 1822
Hand-colored etching
and aquatint
18 ¾ x 26 ½"
(42.19 x 59.63 cm)

A Big Discovery

Audubon came up with a solution to what had been an enduring conundrum for artists: how to make a bird appear lifelike in a painting. The problem was that birds, being flighty, wouldn't sit still long enough to satisfy an artist's needs. Even caged birds move around too much for accurate work, and when Audubon drew from dead models, he found the results lifeless as well. He tried hanging the birds from string and even made a movable mannequin of wood, but discarded it, claiming that it looked like a Dodo. The solution to this problem, which he first attempted with a kingfisher, was an ingenious variation on his experiments with taxidermy: After shooting a bird, he would use wires to attach the model's feet to a gridded board; then, threading more wire through the body, would prop up its neck and tail feathers, getting it to pose as he remembered from nature.

Sound Byte:
"There stood before me a real kingfisher. I outlined the bird with the aid of compasses, then colored and finished it. That was my first drawing actually from nature, for even the model's eye was still as if full of life."
—JOHN JAMES AUDUBON

Snowy Owl
1829
Watercolor
pastel, and
graphite on
paper
37 $\frac{7}{8}$ x 25 $\frac{5}{8}$"
(96.3 x 65 cm)

I Do, I Do

One day while out hunting, Audubon ran into his neighbor, Mr. Bakewell, who invited him to lunch. They arrived to find Bakewell's daughter, **Lucy Bakewell** (1787–1874), sewing in the parlor, and Audubon was immediately smitten. ("Her form showed both grace and beauty," he would later tell his sons. "My heart followed every one of her steps.") The English-descended Lucy felt the same for this dashing, handsome Frenchman, and they married in 1808.

Money in the Pits

Unfortunately, Audubon so mismanaged his Pennsylvania landholdings that the property had to be sold. In 1810, the family moved to Henderson, Kentucky, where Audubon and his business partner, **Ferdinand Rozier**, the son of a friend of Audubon's father, set up a trading business in Sainte Genevieve, Missouri, a village not far from Saint Louis. Unfortunately, the Embargo Act (enacted as a reaction to the Napoleonic Wars) cut off overseas trade, thus ending the business. Audubon dissolved the partnership and opened a general store in Henderson. Successful for a while, he bought

Lucy Audubon
in miniature portrait
by Frederick Cruikshank
1835

some land and built a house. His first child, **Victor Gifford Audubon,** was born June 12, 1809, and his second son, **John Woodhouse Audubon,** on November 30, 1812. He and Lucy later had two daughters, both of whom died early in life.

> *FYI:* **His destroyed paintings**—Audubon had stored about 200 bird paintings in a box left at a friend's farm. The paintings were destroyed by Norway rats, which nested inside the box. Audubon discovered his loss when he returned to Kentucky in 1812. A Japanese woodcut from *The Western Countries Book of Successful Careers,* published in 1878, depicts an astonished Audubon opening the box.

Sound Byte:
"My business went on prosperously when I attended to it. But birds were birds and my thoughts were ever and anon turning towards them as to my greatest delight. Beyond this, I really cared not. I seldom passed a day without drawing a bird or noting something respecting its habits."

—JOHN JAMES AUDUBON, 1828

Audubon started a new partnership with his brother-in-law, Thomas Bakewell, to build a steam-powered mill to grind grain and saw wood. This, too, collapsed. The continual progression of enterprises and

financial setbacks caused Audubon's fiscal affairs to deteriorate to such a degree that he was sent to debtors' prison in 1819. He and Lucy had to sell most of their possessions and declare bankruptcy to secure his release. His lack of business acumen, his early penchant for dressing like a dandy and living like a gentleman, and his preference for drawing birds rather than attempting more lucrative pursuits had magnified his misfortunes.

Sound Byte:

"Without any money, my talents are to be my support and my enthusiasm my guide in my difficulties, the whole of which I am ready to exert, to keep, and to surmount."

—JOHN JAMES AUDUBON, 1820

The Birds' First Flight

Stripped of his assets, Audubon went through a period of depression from which he recovered only through serious resolve. He had already compiled a large group of bird drawings by the time he was released from debtors' prison in 1819, and from that moment forward he dedicated himself to creating an ornithological survey of American birds while trying to earn enough money to support himself and his family. One way he made a living was by drawing chalk portraits, such as the

OPPOSITE
Detail from
American Goldfinch
1824

one of his friend *Nicholas Berthoud* (1819), and by painting birds and animals in oil for quick sale. The portraits sold for between $5.00 and $25.00 and are not unlike those by other portrait practitioners of the Federal period, such as the French-born **Charles Balthazar Julien Févret de Saint-Memin** (1770–1852). The strong profile outlines are also comparable in style to his initial treatment of birds.

OPPOSITE
Detail from
*Cerulean
Warbler*
1822

Audubon's personal goals in documenting North American birds were threefold: to surpass the work of all previous illustrators; to make a name for himself; and, above all, to succeed financially. This dedicated artist-naturalist who spent weeks at a time in the wilderness observing the habits of birds—and searching for new species that would enhance his reputation as a man of science—was also a pragmatist with a family to support.

Sound Byte:
"It is not the naturalist that I wish to please altogether. I assure thee it is the wealthy part of the community. The first can only speak well or ill of me, but the latter will fill my pockets."
—JOHN JAMES AUDUBON, 1826

Yet Another Move

The family moved to Cincinnati in January 1820, where Audubon worked part-time as a taxidermist and painter of backgrounds for the newly opened Western Museum at Cincinnati College. The museum's founder and director, Daniel Drake, was so taken with his new employee's bird illustrations that he hosted the first Audubon exhibition, and introduced the young painter to his natural scientist acquaintances. They were all impressed by both Audubon's artistic talent and the scientific accuracy of his renderings.

To bolster his taxidermy income, Audubon opened a drawing school, which attracted about 25 pupils. Among his students was **Joseph Mason** (1808–1842), whose talent was so remarkable that Audubon took him on as an apprentice. (Eventually, Mason would become part of a team who created the backgrounds for *The Birds of America*.) By this time, Audubon had finished a number of drawings, and his avocation was transformed into his life's work.

And Away We Go!

In an effort to represent birds from across the country, Audubon left Cincinnati to explore the territories southwest of the Missouri River— the beginnings of the American frontier. He dressed the way all frontiersmen did—in buckskin, moccasins, and buffalo robe—and paid for his travels with portrait work and flute performances.

A prolific writer, Audubon kept journals of his experiences from 1822 onward, and wrote hundreds of letters to friends, family, acquaintances, and business associates. Unfortunately, many of his journals were bowdlerized by his granddaughter, but the few that remain untouched reveal a man who could be both sensitive and bawdy, loving and pragmatic, hardworking and a dreamer. He was articulate and engrossing in his ability to record his experiences and express his reactions and emotions in his second language. His letters and journals reveal tenderness for his family and regret for the long periods spent away from them, as well as the writer's difficulty with punctuation (he had mastered the English language and wrote expressively, but lacked some of the finer points of grammar).

FYI: **His nibs**—Audubon preferred quills of trumpeter swans because they were "hard, and yet so elastic, that the best steel pen of the present day might have blushed, if it could, to be compared with them."

Sound Byte:
"I take a bird neatly killed, put him up with wires, and when satisfied with the truth of the position, I take my palette and finish off the bird at one sitting."

—JOHN JAMES AUDUBON

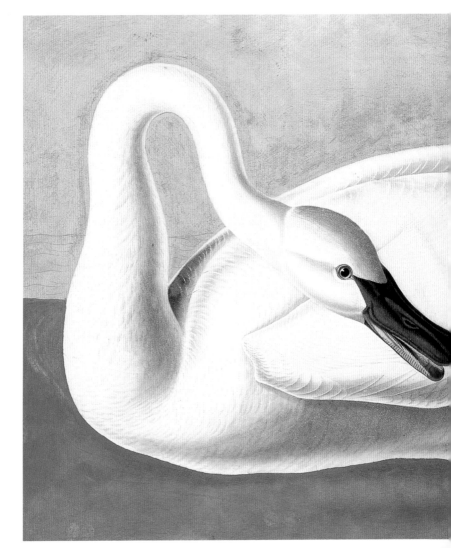

Trumpeter Swan
c. 1836–37
Watercolor, pastel
oil, graphite, and
selected scraping
on paper
23 x 37 ¾"
(51.75 x 84.94 cm)

Feathered Friends

OPPOSITE
Detail from
Northern Parula
1821

The desire to produce a comprehensive book depicting the birds of North America had been stimulated by the less-than-thorough quality of earlier illustrated books, such as *American Ornithology* (1808–14), the first attempt at a comprehensive scientific study of North American birds; it was begun by **Alexander Wilson** (1766–1813) and completed by **Titian Ramsey Peale** (1799–1885) after Wilson's death. Audubon had met Wilson while he was working in Louisville, when Wilson came to town to entice subscribers. Wilson's book was illustrated with hand-colored engravings, as were those by predecessors and contemporaries. Audubon vowed to improve upon earlier static portrayals of birds in profile as well as to represent the birds life-size.

We know that Audubon had read *Travels through North and South Carolina, Georgia, East and West Florida, the Cherokee Country, the Extensive Territories of the Muscogulges, or Creek Confederacy, and the Country of the Chactaws* (1791), by William Bartram (1729–1833), because he had the temerity to criticize it in a moment of overconfidence.

Audubon must also have been influenced by pioneering work being done during this time in the fields of botany and entomology as well as zoology. It was during this time that the classification of quadrupeds, plants, and birds was established. Many books and treatises were published. Prints and watercolors (and natural history) were in their heyday in early 19th-century England, and large collections of natural curiosities were formed, including that of Sir Hans Sloane, whose donations formed the basis of the natural history collection of the British Museum. Charles Darwin himself would eventually become aware of Audubon's work and cite him in his publications.

Principles of "Seriality"

Serialization had been a basic practice since the beginning of print-making in the 15th century. During the 18th century, the production of serial prints was firmly established and was commonly financed in all subjects—fine art as well as natural history—by subscribers. Besides Wilson's *American Ornithology*, Audubon would have been inspired by *The Natural History of Carolina, Florida, and the Bahama Islands*

(1731–43) by the naturalist **Mark Catesby** (1682–1749), which contained 220 etchings of North-American flora and fauna and took 20 years to complete. Shaw's pioneering print series, *Picturesque Views*, was engraved by **John Hill** (1770–1850); it introduced American audiences to the color potential of aquatint engraving. Like many long-term print projects, this one was never completed, for a variety of reasons: excessive expenses, public indifference, the bankruptcy of publishing firms, and Shaw's inability to cover expenses.

However, the unfinished work was reprinted in 1835. By that time the market had improved, due to economic expansion and a growing leisure class, which created a demand for images of American scenery. In 1821, Hill was again called upon, this time to engrave Wall's *Hudson River Portfolio*, 24 hand-colored aquatint engravings, the largest colored landscape prints (14 x 21") to be engraved in the United States at that time. The artist had to take an active role in financing and promoting a publication, but the work often paid off: During the first half of the 19th century, many artists expanded both their reputations and their incomes by having their paintings reproduced as prints. Wall's *Portfolio* was reissued in 1828 and 1834, testimony to its popularity.

Help from American Artists

Because he did not have formal academic training, Audubon continually experimented with different techniques during his formative years, seeking ways to best capture the nuances of color and the texture of feathers and fur of the birds and animals that were his primary subjects. He perfected his ability to translate onto paper a realistic approximation of the wildlife he so keenly observed. In America, he sought advice about painting in oil from several artists, including prominent portraitists such as **John Wesley Jarvis** (1780–1840), **Thomas Sully** (1783–1872), **Henry Inman** (1801–1846), **John Vanderlyn** (1775–1852), and **John Stein**, a less well known portrait painter from Pennsylvania who was active in the 1820s. Interestingly, Stein was probably the artist who inspired **Thomas Cole** (1801–1848), founder of the Hudson River School of landscape painting. Audubon never excelled in oil painting but eventually became an extraordinary watercolorist whose layering of color washes created multicolored effects, density, and depth. This can be seen in *Passenger Pigeon* (1824) and *Carolina Parakeets* (1825), pictures of two species abundant in Audubon's time but now extinct.

Sound Byte:

"Doubtless, the reader will say, while looking at the seven figures of Parakeets represented in the plate, that I spared not my labour. I never do, so anxious am I to promote his pleasure."

—JOHN JAMES AUDUBON

Passenger Pigeon
1824
Watercolor
gouache, graphite
pastel, and black
chalk (?) on paper
26 ³/₁₆ x 18 ¹/₄"
(66.5 x 46.4 cm)
Painted in
Pittsburgh
Pennsylvania

Carolina Parakeets
1825
Watercolor
graphite, gouache
crayon/pastel, and
glazing on paper
29 11/16 x 21 3/16"
(75.4 x 53.9 cm)
Painted in
Louisiana

It was in 1824, after he had completed a number of watercolors, that Audubon went to Philadelphia to seek an engraver for his bird series. Philadelphia was then the intellectual and scientific hub of the United States as well as a center for publishing. Audubon must have known of, or met, **Charles Willson Peale** (1741–1827), the renowned artist-naturalist who, in 1786, had opened the first museum in the United States. There, visitors were exposed to natural-history specimens displayed along with portraits of American heroes and presidents, and the *Exhumation of the American Mastodon*, which Peale had painted in 1806–08. We know that Audubon was acquainted with two of Peale's artist sons, Titian and **Rembrandt Peale** (1778–1860). Titian was at this time completing *American Ornithology*, which one of Audubon's predecessors, Alexander Wilson, had left unfinished at the time of his death.

Not So Lucky

Because of his somewhat brazen and cocky personality, his back-woodsman appearance, his lack of a formal background in science, and primarily because of competition from the supporters of Wilson's bird book, Audubon was rebuffed by most of the scientific community as well as by publishers in Philadelphia and New York. The prominent American naturalist **George Ord**—a long-time friend of Alexander Wilson's and collaborator on *American Ornithology*—was incensed by the appearance that Audubon was trying to take over Wilson's turf.

He accused Audubon of plagiarism and scientific error, and made sure that none of Philadelphia's scientific societies (or socially prominent collectors) would have anything to do with *The Birds*.

Encouraged by a few supporters—including Napoleon's nephew, **Charles Lucien Bonaparte** (1803–1857), who had published a book on birds in the America that was not included in Wilson's *American Ornithology*—Audubon decided to take his drawings to England.

Sound Byte:
"If I were jealous, I would have a bitter time of it, for every bird is my rival."
—LUCY BAKEWELL AUDUBON, n.d.

Publishing *The Birds of America*

Prior to leaving for Liverpool, Audubon did not have a set plan, but he soon devised a strategy to publish *The Birds of America* through subscriptions on the installment plan. According to his first prospectus, Audubon initially intended to publish 400 life-size images of the birds of North America, showing differences between males, females, and young, and documenting their food and natural habitats—the perfect merger of art and science. The images were to be etched in aquatint on fine-quality Whatman paper, composed of linen and cotton fibers, measuring 29 ½ x 39 ½"—called double-elephant sheets, the largest size available at that time. (Whatman paper was produced by a specific English paper mill. We know this by the watermarks.) They were to be produced in 80 *fascicles*, called numbers or parts, each installment containing one large bird, such as the Gyrfalcon, one medium-size bird, such as the Whippoorwill, and three small birds, such as the Cerulean Warbler, where the background is painted by Audubon's young student, Joseph Mason.

The First Touch of Fame

Armed with letters of introduction, Audubon arrived in Liverpool on July 21, 1826. A letter from a friend to the merchant **Richard Rathbone** (1788–1860), a man of wealth and influence, was the artist's principal asset (along with his taste for theatrics and self-promotion). The Rathbone family took it upon themselves to help Audubon in his difficult, long-term project, and became his greatest champions. They introduced him to influential scientists, patrons of the arts, and printers, all of whom agreed that Audubon's work was worthy of full-size reproduction by a master engraver. Within 11 days, his beautiful watercolors were being exhibited at the Liverpool Royal Institution.

And at the Same Time...

At the time Audubon arrived in England, the horse portraits of

Gyrfalcon
1837
Watercolor
graphite, gouache
glazing, and
scraping on paper
38 $\frac{1}{2}$ x 25 $\frac{5}{8}$"
(97.8 x 65.2 cm)
Painted in
Great Britain

Whippoorwill
c. 1827-30
Watercolor
graphite, and
selected glazing
on paper
28 ¹³/₁₆ x 21 ¹/₂"
(73.2 x 54.6 cm)
Probably painted
in New Jersey

Cerulean Warbler
1822
Watercolor
graphite, gouache
(black) pastel/chalk
and glazing on
paper
18 7/8 x 11 3/4"
(47.9 x 29.8 cm)
Probably painted in
Louisiana or
Mississippi

George Stubbs (1724–1806), the romantic animal paintings of **Sir Edwin Landseer** (1802–1873), the early work of the multifaceted **Edward Lear** (1812–1888), as well as the oils and watercolors of the renowned **Joseph Mallord William Turner** (1775–1851), were often on view at the Royal Academy or hung in the houses of some of Audubon's patrons. They were widely available as prints. Turner, for example, produced a collection of closely scrutinized bird drawings for his patrons the Fawkes family at Farnley Hall in Yorkshire, England; his drawings reveal the virtuosity of his watercolor technique but do not show a real understanding of the structure of the individual species.

At the same time, 19-year-old Edward Lear published his first book, *Illustrations of the Family of Psittacidae, or Parrots.* He also worked on the famous *Birds of Europe* by John Gould (1804–1881). Lear's bold and accurate drawings of birds and animals were often compared to those of Audubon, but by the time Lear was 25, he had abandoned his ornithological work to devote himself to landscape painting. (And yes, he is the same Edward Lear known for his poems, *A Book of Nonsense.*)

George Stubbs, best known for his precise horse portraits, saw some of his images incorporated into natural-history books and even produced his own etched illustrations in *The Anatomy of the Horse* in 1766. Sir Edwin Landseer, one of the most popular artists of the early Victorian period, specialized in romantic pictures of animals, anthropomorphizing his subjects in a manner that can be compared to that of Audubon.

A Hit with the Brits

While Americans shunned Audubon because of his long, flowing hair preened with bear grease, his provincial pantaloons, his animal-skin jacket, and his arrogance, the English (having just been introduced to noble frontiersman Natty Bumppo in James Fenimore Cooper's novel *The Pioneers*, 1823) were fascinated by his wild American manners and apparel. It was a classic story of the New World: An immigrant with a French accent, who had been an American citizen only since 1812, was received in Europe a mere 14 years later as the quintessential American frontiersman. (At a moment's notice, however, Audubon would replace his wolfskin coat with an English greatcoat if doing so held the promise of a sale.) Before leaving Liverpool for London, he had cut his hair in the European style. He skipped the bear grease, wore a formal hat, and carried a sword cane, all the while complaining of "the finery with which I made a popinjay of myself in my youth." During a trip to Paris, he went to the Louvre museum wearing a beaver hat, and the doorman refused him entry.

Sound Byte:
"This day my hair was sacrificed, and the will of God usurped by the wishes of man."

—JOHN JAMES AUDUBON, March 19, 1827, diary notation about cutting his hair to please a potential patron

Wild Turkey
c. 1825
Watercolor
graphite on
paper

Moving Right Along...

By November 1826, Audubon had reached an agreement with the respected Edinburgh engraver **William Home Lizars** (1788–1859). Working with Lizars, Audubon produced ten superb prints in a short time, of which *Wild Turkey* was the first. By June 1827, Lizars was forced to stop because of a strike by his colorists but, luckily, Audubon soon found an even better engraver in the **Robert Havells**—Senior and Junior—with Junior (1783–1878) retouching the ten plates Lizars had completed and staying with the project for its 11-year duration. The Havells charged less than Lizars, and, because their shop was located in London, Audubon no longer had to pay to ship the Whatman paper to Edinburgh, making *The Birds* all the more profitable.

Between England and America

Between 1826 and 1838, Audubon produced at least half of the watercolors, wrote and published the *Ornithological Biography* (the five-volume text that accompanied the prints), crossed the ocean four times, and traveled from the Florida Keys to Labrador in search of new species of birds, some of which are no longer extant. Although the White-Crowned Pigeon was wantonly slaughtered, it is still in existence, which cannot be said of the Passenger Pigeon, the last of which died in captivity in 1914. The beautiful Carolina Parakeet, the only parrot native to the United States, suffered a similar fate, killed for its decorative feathers and because it was an annoyance to farmers. Audubon documented the habits of these gorgeous birds and portrayed their brilliantly colored feathers in one of his most intricately designed compositions.

Key west Pigeon.
COLUMBA MONTANA

Key West Quail-Dove
1832
Hand-colored etching and aquatint
20 3/4 x 25 7/8" (57.4 x 65.7 cm)

Sound Byte:

"Perhaps the first year after thou art with me will not be quite so comfortable as I could wish it, but we will be together and thou wilt be of immense help and assistance in my business in ways I cannot well explain."

—JOHN JAMES AUDUBON, December 26, 1827, in a letter to his wife

At one point, the Passenger Pigeon was more common than any other bird in America—so much so that it was actually deemed a pest. Members of hunting parties found it hard to miss, and so many were shot that at times people ate nothing but pigeon for weeks. Audubon's painting shows them billing (i.e., the female regurgitating food into the mouth of the brightly colored male), which appears to the human eye as a gesture of striking tenderness and affection, a kind of French kiss. The forms of the two birds are so entwined that they form a harmonious curve with the branches they stand on and the birds seem devotedly, hopelessly in love. That Audubon could evoke such rich, engaging drama and emotion from animals is a major key to his enduring status and popularity as an artist.

Audubon also depicted the White-Crowned Pigeon in the act of billing. He painted these birds at Indian Key, Florida, in April 1832, camouflaged by the Geiger tree in which they perch. The tree was painted by his assistant at the time, **George Lehman** (c. 1800–1870). Though Audubon would become a master at conveying the literal tex-

OPPOSITE
Detail from
White-Crowned Pigeon
1832
Watercolor
graphite
gouache
pastel (?)
collage, glazing
on paper
29 ³/₁₆ x 21"
(74.2 x 53.4 cm)

ture of feathers, he could also be intensely romantic, as in this portrait, where the pair seem enrobed in blue velvet. It was during this trip south that Audubon first met the amateur naturalist **Rev. John Bachman** (1790–1874), with whom he worked on his last large project, *The Quadrupeds*, and whose daughters his sons married. In addition to Audubon's family, the Rev. Bachman would become Audubon's most important ally and partner in the later years of his life.

Back in England, Audubon was unsuccessful in convincing his wife to join him there, so he returned to America in April of 1829 to do more drawings, to find more subscribers, and to promote his work through exhibitions. He returned to England with Lucy in April of 1830.

> *FYI:* **The Wiring Technique**—When Audubon demonstrated his wiring technique to European scientific societies in the 1820s, he was greeted across the continent by standing ovations.

Sound Byte:
"It seems, as if as long as I live, I must labour as if at the treadmill…. I wish I had eight pairs of hands."
—JOHN JAMES AUDUBON, 1829

A Supportive Wife

Fortunately, Audubon had the complete backing and extensive help of his wife, Lucy, who relieved him of his familial responsibilities and allowed him to single-mindedly pursue his passion. Without the help of this pioneer woman, who virtually brought up and supported their sons on her own, Audubon's masterwork might never have reached the light of day. When his sons, John Woodhouse and Victor Gifford, came of age, they helped their father supervise the production, sales, and collections of payments, and also assisted in the actual painting, adding backgrounds and perhaps an occasional bird. Eventually they took over subsequent projects, and the family business became their vocation as well.

OPPOSITE
Great Gray Owl
c. 1834-36
Watercolor
graphite, brown
and black pastel
on paper
34 $^{3}/_{16}$ x 25 $^{1}/_{8}$"
(86.8 x 63.8 cm)
Painted probably in
London, England

Sound Byte:
"My wife determined that my genius should prevail, and that my final success as an ornithologist should be triumphant."
—JOHN JAMES AUDUBON

Creating the Images

In creating the paintings that the engraver would follow in printing the bird series, Audubon would first lay out an entire composition in graphite using a light underdrawing barely visible beneath the paint.

Even when the background was completed by an assistant, the total conception was, for the most part, Audubon's. Toward the end of the project, expediency was necessary, and Audubon relied on written instructions to Havell such as that found on the *Great Gray Owl*, instructing him to raise the bird about four inches in the copper plate and to add a landscape below of wild mountains and woods (in this case, Havell did not follow Audubon's background recommendations in the print). The birds were often completed first by Audubon, with the backgrounds being added later by assistants; there is evidence, however, of instances where the background was painted first, as in the *Northern Parula*. The stem of the flower, painted by Audubon's young assistant, Joseph Mason, can be seen as a *pentimento* (i.e., an element that has been painted over but reappears with time) through the body of the bird.

The Painter's Painters

In addition to the Havells and Audubon's sons, three artists assisted Audubon in the painting of images for *The Birds of America*: Joseph Mason, George Lehman, and **Maria Martin** (1796–1863). A fourth, the Scottish artist **Joseph Bartholomew Kidd** (1808–1889), was hired to copy Audubon's watercolors in oils for exhibition and sale, but he did not participate in the actual print series. The use of assistants was a time-honored practice and their work traditionally remained unacknowledged, which sometimes caused disagreements. Joseph Mason

spent two years working with Audubon and became known for flower pictures and portraits (Audubon said that Mason drew flowers "better than any man probably in America"). Afterward, Mason charged that Audubon did not credit his work properly.

Lehman worked with Audubon between 1831 and 1832, and his hand is clearly discernible in many of Audubon's drawings of shorebirds, such as the *Long-Billed Curlew*, which pictures the city of Charleston in the background. After he left Audubon's employ, Lehman formed two prominent Philadelphia lithography firms and painted and printed scenes of notable events and portraits of celebrities, including the popular frontiersman Davy Crockett.

A Talented Woman Enters the Picture

Audubon met the gifted amateur water-

Long-Billed Curlew
1831
Watercolor, pastel graphite, gouache glazing, and scraping on paper
24 $^{15}/_{16}$ x 37 $^{5}/_{8}$"
(63.4 x 95.7 cm)
Painted in Charleston South Carolina

colorist Maria Martin in 1831. Martin specialized in botanical subjects and assisted Audubon on the floral backgrounds for a number of his later works. Her brother-in-law (and later her husband), the Rev. John Bachman, provided skins and scientific text as well as focus and drive when Audubon began to deteriorate mentally. Perhaps because Martin was a woman, Audubon was able to express his sincere appreciation and admiration of her work more easily than he had to his other assistants. He named a painting *Maria's Woodpecker* in tribute to her.

Sound Byte:
"I feel bound to make some ornithological acknowledgement for the aid she has on several occasions afforded me in embellishing my drawings of birds, by adding to them beautiful and correct representations of plants and flowers."
—JOHN JAMES AUDUBON, 1839

Audubon the Artist

Audubon's earliest drawings are stiff, unanimated specimens rendered in pastel and graphite, birds in profile placed centrally on the page, standing on what could be called a primal clump of earth, as in *Bonaparte's Gull*, or clutching a lichen-covered tree branch, as seen in the *Sharp-Shinned Hawk* (see page 107).

As he matured, Audubon experimented not only with ways for setting

Bonaparte's Gull
1820
Watercolor, pastel
graphite with
brown ink
inscriptions
26 x 22"
(58.5 x 49.5 cm)

up his models but also with his technique for depicting the nuances of texture and color, the iridescence of feathers, the appearance of soft down, the reflection of light, and the overall look of the living birds. At first, he drew directly from nature and finished the work from dead specimens. Later, as mentioned previously, he tried other methods until he finally found that by threading wire through a freshly killed bird he could fix it into positions he had observed in nature. By placing the wired bird on a gridded board, he was able to transpose the drama and action of real life onto paper.

As his style and expertise evolved, Audubon increasingly animated his subjects, giving them human qualities: The painting *Great Cormorant* (1833–34) shows young chicks being cared for by their parents, who feed them regurgitated food. Audubon noted that the young ate more than their weight each day and were always ready for more. These birds, painted in Labrador, are shown as a family rather than in their more common posture as expert fish catchers, exploited for their prowess by fisherman in Europe and Asia. Perhaps Audubon, alone on the sterile and stormy coast of Labrador and nostalgic for his own family, pictured them as he himself yearned to be.

Some of Audubon's most powerful and accomplished pictures, such as *Roseate Spoonbill*, were produced in the late 1820s and early 1830s, when he was at the height of his artistic career. The watercolor of the

OPPOSITE
Detail from
*Great
Cormorant*
1833 and 1834
Watercolor
graphite
gouache
glazing on paper
25 $\frac{1}{2}$ x 38 $\frac{1}{2}$"
(64.9 x 97.8 cm)
Painted in
Labrador

OVERLEAF
Roseate Spoonbill
c. 1831-32
Watercolor
graphite, glazing
and gouache
on paper
23 $\frac{1}{8}$ x 35 $\frac{11}{16}$"
(58.7 x 90.6 cm)

Spoonbill is unfinished, but enough was sketched in for Havell to be able to complete the background in the engraving as the artist intended.

Audubon became so proficient that even when he couldn't observe the bird directly and had to work from notes and skins alone, he could make the image seem as though it had been drawn from life. This can be seen in the *Great Gray Owl* (c. 1834–36), a startling improvement over the early stilted efforts. Part of his success was due to the young Havell, who was an artist in his own right and seemed to have an instinctive understanding of Audubon's aesthetic standards. In addition to executing the engraved plates, Havell junior also oversaw the work of the colorists, mostly women, who worked in groups from Audubon's watercolor (there were times, however, when Audubon berated Havell for a lack of consistency in color from print to print).

A Quick Word on Watercolors

Watercolors are ground pigments mixed in a water-soluble substance with gum arabic as the binding agent. They are traditionally applied with brushes to paper, silk, ivory, linen, and other supports. They can be prepared in solid dry cakes or semifluid in tubes. Watercolor was in its heyday in England during the first half of the 19th century and moved to America 50 years later. In 1866, the American Society of Painters in Water Colors was founded and was eventually renamed the American Water Color Society. The medium reached its apex from the 1870s on, when many important American artists, including **Thomas Eakins** (1844–1916), **Winslow Homer** (1836–1910), and **John Singer Sargent** (1856–1925), utilized it for its immediacy, its transparency, and its portability. Large, finished watercolors, sometimes simulating aspects of oil painting, were frequently shown alongside oil paintings at art exhibitions.

One of the most interesting characteristics of Audubon's watercolors is the asymmetry of his compositions. This oriental-like aesthetic is visible, for example, in the diagonal emphasis of the *Magnolia Warbler* (1829), the off-center placement on the page in the *American Goldfinch* (1824), the cropping of the branch on which the *Tufted Titmouse* (1822) plays, and the simplification of form as in the *Common Tern*, first painted in 1821 and revised around 1834. These features, reminiscent of earlier Japanese, Chinese, and Indian pictures of nature, could be seen in prints,

Black & Yellow Warbler. male.
Sylvia maculosa.

Great Pine Swamp
Aug 2 18
J.J.A.

Crested Titmouse Male 1. F 2.
Parus bicolor.
Plant Pinus Strobus.

N.º 8. Plate 39.

porcelain, and the decorated furniture found in upper-class houses in England and in the homes and plantations of wealthy families in and around Philadelphia and New Orleans. The skewed compositions of the paintings are not as apparent in the prints, because the backgrounds fill in the empty spaces and frequently camouflage the asymmetry and cropping.

The Human Animal

Audubon and a number of British artists were products of their age: They were fascinated by natural history and they saw human qualities in animal behavior. Landseer's *Jocko with a Hedgehog*, exhibited at the Royal Academy in 1827, and Audubon's *Brown Thrasher* (1829), showing birds defending the eggs in their nest against the invasion of a black snake, are strikingly human. Audubon meant to inspire compassion and sympathy from the viewer, and the accompanying text served to reinforce the lesson of how, by joining forces, a common enemy can be defeated.

The Birds of America was published from 1827 to 1838. Twenty-five prints were to be published annually and delivered in tin cases at $1,000 per set, a high price even for people of means like the Baron Nathan M. Rothschild (who balked at the cost). Subscribers would sign up for the entire series but pay in installments on receiving each set. The project was financed by their payments, each installment funding the next group of prints. Subscribers were also advised to

OPPOSITE LEFT
Common Tern
c. 1834
Watercolor
graphite, and
gouache (on
beak) on paper
21 $^1/_2$ x 14 $^5/_8$"
(54.6 x 37.3 cm)

OPPOSITE RIGHT
Tufted Titmouse
1822
Watercolor
graphite
gouache, and
glazing on paper
18 $^5/_8$ x 11 $^5/_8$"
(47.3 x 29.5 cm)
Painted in
Louisiana or
Mississippi

Brown Thrasher
1829
Watercolor
pastel, graphite
scraping
on paper
37 $^{11}/_{16}$ x 25"
(95.8 x 63.6 cm)
Painted on the
East Coast of
the United States

purchase portfolios or have the prints bound into four volumes at an additional cost. Because of ongoing discoveries of new species, Audubon added seven numbers at the end, making a total of 87 parts containing 435 plates. This represents 1,065 individual birds and 457 species. The first three volumes comprised 100 prints each, and the last contained an extra 35 because of the addition of newly discovered species.

FYI: **Sets of The Birds**—It is not known exactly how many full sets of the series were actually completed, but the estimates by experts have ranged from between 185 and 200 to perhaps as many as 223. As of this writing, only 170 have secure records, fewer than 119 remain intact, and many of those have damaged prints. Because of the increased value of these rare and beautiful images, the sets are often broken up and the prints sold individually.

In the end, Audubon wanted to add even more birds, but most subscribers during the economic depression of 1836 and 1837 failed to agree. Instead, in order to accommodate recent discoveries, Audubon made several composite arrangements in the final volume, placing on a single page several related species, such as Maria's Woodpecker, Three-Toed Woodpecker, Phillips Woodpecker, Canadian Woodpecker, Harris's Woodpecker, and Audubon's Woodpecker. This was the one case in which Audubon, who rarely compromised his standards because of cost or complexity, altered his original plan to comply with consumer demand.

Golden–Winged,
Cape May, Black–
Throated Green
Blackburnian
MacGillivray's
Warblers
1836–37
Watercolor
Graphite, traces of
black pastel
on paper
$21^{7}/_{8}$ x $14^{1}/_{2}$"
(55.5 x 36.7 cm)
Painted in
Charleston, South
Carolina

Red-Bellied Woodpecker Northern Flicker Yellow-Bellied Sapsucker, Lewis's Woodpecker, and Hairy Woodpecker
Upper four birds painted c. 1822; painting completed in Charleston South Carolina during the winter of 1836-37
Watercolor, pastel graphite, gouache collage, and glazing on paper
37 ⅛ x 24 ¼"
(94.3 x 61.7 cm)

John James
Audubon's
portable lap desk
Mahogany
folding

Great Scot!

Because of his frenetic schedule and his limited scientific background, Audubon hired the Scottish scientist **William MacGillivray** (1796– 1852) to edit his *Ornithological Biography* and supply scientific details for his descriptions of the habits and habitats of the birds. He included "Episodes," a mix of reality and fiction about the wilderness based on his own or his acquaintances' experiences.

The expenses Audubon incurred for his great project were in some respects immeasurable. His outlay for travel and the cost of his forays into the wilderness cannot be adequately assessed; he had to pay William MacGillivray for editing; his assistants Joseph Mason, George Lehman, and Maria Martin; Joseph Bartholomew Kidd, who copied his work in oil; Henry Ward, his taxidermist; and, finally, the engravers and colorists. Booksellers who sold the folios received commissions, and the artist supplied the materials for printing—copper plates, paper, and paints. This was an expensive undertaking for a single individual, and Audubon was never able to find long-range national or institutional backing. Of necessity, he became a one-man marketing machine.

Audubon, the Promoter of Birds

In addition to creating, producing, and publishing the series, Audubon also served as his own best promoter. His success was ensured by his enthusiasm for the product and his unrelenting persistence. Besides the work itself, Audubon's constant preoccupation was to attract subscribers, and only someone with his energy, drive, and compulsive dedication could have succeeded with this massive project.

Pitching to the Bigwigs

Following the conventional marketing rationale of his time, Audubon obtained letters of introduction from anyone who might know a prospective buyer. He exploited such personal contacts as Charles

Lucien Bonaparte, DeWitt Clinton, Henry Clay, and Andrew Jackson to meet other celebrities and royalty, and if these new contacts wouldn't agree to subscribe, he would ask permission to publish their names as endorsers in his constantly updated prospectus. He secured the patronage of the English royal family and other members of the nobility—eventually receiving subscriptions from England's King George IV, France's King Charles X, and the Duke of Orleans. Statesmen such as **Daniel Webster** (1782–1852) and institutions such as the Library of Congress and the Harvard University Library also signed on.

Audubon exhibited his watercolors and prints as a form of advertising, sometimes charging an admission fee to help defray expenses. His paintings were shown in Paris, London, Edinburgh, and Liverpool. Although the paintings were created primarily to serve as models for the engraver and colorists, the artist additionally valued them as works of art, as we do today. Audubon even showed his work at his lodgings, complaining that he became "tired out holding up drawings…all day."

Scoring Big with Exhibitions

The exhibits were wildly successful. One London critic wrote, "Their plumages sparkle with nature's own tints; you see them in motion or at rest, in their play and in their combats, in their anger fits and their caresses, singing, running, asleep, just awakened, beating the air, skimming the waves or rending one another in their battles…a vision of the New World."

Newspapers not only advertised his work but also featured articles, interesting letters, and stories about his adventures. Excerpts from his own prodigious writings were published serially; his bravery and endurance in search of new birds and his progress in producing the prints made good copy. Editors and reporters expanded, dramatized, and glorified the reputation of this appealing, romantic figure, making him a media hero in his day.

Sound Byte:

"This distinguished ornithologist has been the object of a general interest among the most intelligent classes of society, during his visit to this city. His pictures of the different kinds of wild-fowl are greatly admired. They are full of spirit and animation.... His exhibitions of paintings have been thronged with beauty and fashion.... Every public institution should possess itself of his costly and superb work."
—THE NEW-YORK MIRROR, April 20, 1833

Scientific organizations provided Audubon with contacts, exhibition space, and prospective clients. While he always had critics, he was able to convince most naturalists that his work was based on careful observation. Occasionally he made mistakes, as when he identified a juvenile bald eagle as a new species he called the "Bird of Washington." Although he sometimes put birds in awkward positions in order to fit them on the

Whooping Crane
1821-22
Watercolor, oil
paint, graphite
gouache, glazing
and pastel
on paper
37 1/4 x 25 11/16"
(94.7 x 65.2 cm)
Painted in
New Orleans
Louisiana

page, the poses he chose were usually plausible ones, as with the Whooping Crane, the tallest bird in North America, and the Great White Heron (aka Great Blue Heron), where the beak extends into the margin of the print.

A Grueling Workday

To achieve all this, Audubon followed an exhausting schedule. He now had four jobs—ornithologist, painter, publisher, and traveling salesman—and usually rose before dawn and often traveled great distances to meet new people in various cities. Much of his time was spent extolling the importance of the project at dinners and at meetings of scientific societies. Invitations to social events catapulted him into association with upper-class society, people with the necessary means to become subscribers. Drawing was one thing; getting subscribers was real work!

Sound Byte:
"The great round of Company I am thrown in has become fatiguing to me in the extreme and does not agree with my early habits. I go to dine out at 6, 7, or 8 o'clock in the evening and it is one or two in the morning when the party breaks up, then painting all day with my Correspondence that increases daily. My Head is like a Hornet's nest and my body is wearied beyond calculation—yet it has to be done. I cannot refuse a single invitation."
—JOHN JAMES AUDUBON, in a letter to Lucy, December 21, 1826

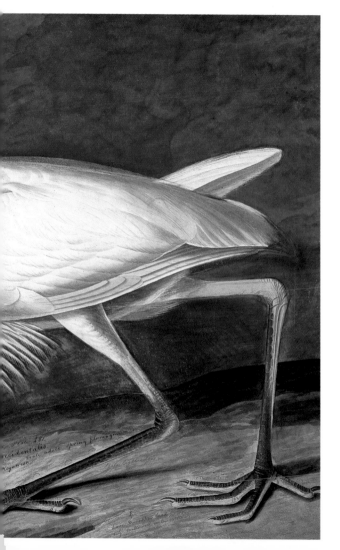

*Great White Heron (*aka *Great Blue Heron).* 1832
Watercolor, pastel graphite, gouache and scraping
on paper
25 $\frac{11}{16}$ x 38 $\frac{5}{16}$"
(65.2 x 98.7 cm)
Painted in
Key West
Florida

A perfectionist, Audubon sometimes drew the same bird several times before he was satisfied. When pushed for time, he incorporated earlier drawings, cutting out images he wished to reuse and pasting them onto the new sheet, as he did in one of his least satisfying pieces, the *Northern Goshawk, Cooper's Hawk*, a composite of artwork from 1809 to 1829. Audubon was among the first artists to incorporate collage consistently, using it to make improvements and correct areas he wanted to cover, integrating the additions as in the *Black Vulture* and the *Great Egret*, where the neck is pasted over.

Sound Byte:

"[We engaged in] measuring, weighing, comparing, and dissecting the birds we had procured; operations which were carried on with the aid of a number of candles thrust into the necks of bottles. Here one examined the flowers and leaves of a plant, there another explored the recesses of a Diver's gullet, while a third skinned a Gull or a Grouse.... Before a month had elapsed, the spoils of many a fine bird hung around the hold; shrubs and flowers were in the press, and I had several drawings finished.... Large jars were filling apace with the bodies of rare birds, fishes, quadrupeds and reptiles, as well as molluscous animals. We had several pets too. Gulls, Cormorants, Guillemots, Puffins, Hawks, and a Raven."

—JOHN JAMES AUDUBON, 1833

Northern Goshawk, Cooper's Hawk 1809 and 1810-19 Watercolor pastel, graphite gouache, and scraping on paper 39 x 25 ⁷/₈" (99 x 65.7 cm) Painted in Kentucky

Audubon shot a large number of specimens, from which he selected the finest—adult males and females, or young chicks. Freshness was important for accurate rendition of colors and iridescence, which fade after death, requiring that the artist work as rapidly as possible. He examined details such as the tongue, wings, and beak, and carefully measured the specimen, regularly noting the sizes on the front and or the back of the sheet. In some instances, a detail not easily seen in the main drawing is shown on the side or below, as in the *Magnificent Frigatebird*.

A Passion for Watercolor

Just as he finally found a method of working with his models, so he perfected a style that satisfied his objective to portray wildlife in the most naturalistic manner possible. He evolved from using pastel and graphite alone to mixing several mediums: watercolor, gouache, oil paint, metallic paint, chalk, ink, and glazes, which he combined with graphite and pastel and even collage. As time went on, probably by the early 1820s, his predominant medium became watercolor, which he layered and mixed with other mediums to achieve complex coloring and depth.

In the *Great Gray Owl* (see page 54), he varied the shades of one color—brown—to reveal the subtle markings of plumage, while in the *Magnificent Frigatebird*, he nuanced and made richer the black pigment by using blue pastel highlights and graphite over the painted surface to delineate feathers. The graphite added iridescence. Since Audubon was experienced with pastel, he would often revert to pastel alone to simulate down feathers, as he did in the baby *Turkey Vulture* (c. 1820), an image that was never published in *The Birds of America*.

Magnificent Frigatebird
1832
Watercolor and graphite on paper
38 ¹/₈ x 25 ¹/₈"
(97 x 64 cm)
Painted in the Florida Keys

OPPOSITE
Turkey Vulture
c. 1820
Watercolor, pastel graphite, and gouache (in beak) on paper
18 5/8 x 18 5/16"
(74.3 x 54.2 cm)
Painted in Charleston South Carolina

While Audubon shot numerous birds, both to procure perfect specimens for his work and for food (gamely noting the taste in his letters and journals), he eventually realized that the wilderness and its abundant game could easily be decimated. Audubon used the metaphor of the ax, just as Thomas Cole and other American artists had done in their paintings, to emphasize the ravages on the wilderness in the name of cultivation. Although Audubon could not be called an ardent preservationist—his skill at hunting alone made him an ironic choice to inspire The Audubon Society (see page 109)—he did, as time went on, realize that measures had to be taken to conserve wildlife.

Sound Byte:
"When I…call back to my mind the grandeur and beauty of those almost uninhabited shores…the dense and lofty summits of forests…unmolested by the axe of the settler…. When I remember that…extraordinary changes have taken place in the short period of twenty years…for the better or for the worse…I feel with regret that there are on record no satisfactory accounts of the state…of the country, from the time when our people first settled it."
—JOHN JAMES AUDUBON, 1808

The Near-Extinction of Species

Audubon documented not only birds and animals but also their natural habitats, recording on paper the beauty of the country as well as the encroachment of civilization. *Snowy Egret* (1832), set near a plantation in the wilderness, reveals a hunter, possibly Audubon himself, aiming at the bird (the background of this watercolor was painted to Audubon's specifications by his assistant, George Lehman). Within a few decades, the egret's luxurious plumes would become wildly popular as accents for women's hats, and the species would be slaughtered in huge numbers, sending it to near-extinction. In Audubon's time, however, these birds were considered culinary delicacies, so the picture's tiny hunter is either in pursuit of a mounted specimen to draw from, or looking to bring dinner home to the family.

A Final Series

In 1839, after obtaining many important subscriptions in Europe, Audubon returned to the United States to work on two new projects while continuing his search for additional subscribers to *The Birds of America*. The other series turned out to be his final one, *The Viviparous Quadrupeds of North America*. In it, he documented the mammals on the continent, and would publish the series between 1851 and 1854 in imperial folio size, 22 x 28". The other project was a smaller version of *The Birds of America* in royal octavo size, 6 ½ x 10" (one-eighth the

Snowy Egret
1832
Watercolor
graphite, gouache
glazing, and
scraping on paper
29 $\frac{1}{4}$ x 21 $\frac{5}{16}$"
(74.3 x 54.2 cm)
Painted in
Charleston
South Carolina

size of the original). The fame he achieved in Europe spread to his adopted country, where he was welcomed by President Andrew Jackson and where he subsequently found an additional 87 subscribers to the original series.

As time went on, Audubon's finances improved, and he lived, as he called it in a letter to Bachman on November 12, 1843, in "the lap of comfort." Yet he never became wealthy from his publications.

Fame in His Own Time

The octavo edition of *The Birds of America*, published by John T. Bowen in Philadelphia and New York between 1840 and 1844, consisted of 500 lithograph plates organized by species. These hand-colored prints were issued in 100 parts of five prints each and bound into seven volumes. Priced at one dollar each or $100 for the entire series, they made Audubon's work available to a far wider audience. John Woodhouse Audubon not only added new birds and changed some compositions to accommodate the smaller size, but was also responsible for copying the original watercolors with the aid of a *camera lucida*, a device that projected the image in a reduced size onto the lithographic stone.

Between 1840 and the 1870s, at least seven octavo editions of *The Birds of America* were printed, a testament to their popularity. By making his great work available to the public in a smaller, less expensive edition, Audubon made even more money than he had from the double-

William Rickarby Miller
Minnie's Land
the Audubon residence on West 155th Street Carmansville, on the Hudson River New York. 1865
Lithograph

elephant folio and proved that there was a serious American audience for the visual arts and natural history.

> *FYI:* **Reproductions**—After Audubon's death, his son John Woodhouse attempted to reissue *The Birds of America* in its original size in *chromo-lithography* (i.e., printing in color). Of the 450 plates planned, Julius Bien, a New York lithographer, completed only 105 plates by 1860. The price of each number was $11, making the total cost much less than that of the original double-elephant folio prints. Chromolithography was new to the United States in the 1840s and Bien's reproductions were a major accomplishment, but completion had to be abandoned because of the Civil War.

A Family Affair

From about 1840 on, Audubon devoted long hours each day to procuring animal specimens and painting them. In 1841, he bought a 35-acre tract of land on the Hudson River, which he called Minnie's Land, incorporating the Scottish word for mother, a term of endearment the family used for Lucy. There, he built a house large enough for himself and his family, and set aside a room as a little studio in which to work.

Sound Byte:

"In one corner stood a painter's easel, with a half-finished sketch of a beaver on paper; in the other lay a skin of an American Panther. The antlers of elks hung upon the walls, stuffed birds of every description of gay plumage ornamented the mantle-piece; and exquisite drawings of field-mice, orioles, and woodpeckers were scattered promiscuously in other parts of the room."

—F. H. HERRICK, describing Audubon's studio in *Audubon the Naturalist*, 1917

The family business became further linked when Audubon's sons married the daughters of John Bachman, **Maria** and **Eliza**. While each son had asssisted in drawing backgrounds and occasionally figures in *The Birds of America*, they were actually coproducers of *The Quadrupeds*. Victor provided many of the backgrounds at the same time as he attended to the business aspects and supervised the production. John

Victor Gifford Audubon and
John Woodhouse Audubon
John James Audubon
1841. Oil on canvas
44 x 60" (98 x 135 cm)

Woodhouse spent almost a year working from specimens in the British Museum, and painted about half of the animals for the imperial folio.

Audubon's Sons

Audubon's sons also maintained independent careers, and both were elected to the National Academy of Design, where they exhibited frequently between 1840 and 1862. Victor was primarily a landscapist, and John a portrait painter who sometimes did animals. They collaborated at times, as for example on the portrait of their father, created around 1841. When Audubon could no longer motivate his sons, it was his coauthor and their father-in-law, John Bachman, whose persistence and perseverance prevailed. Maria Martin, who became Bachman's second wife, assisted them with the drawing of plants, insects, and sometimes animals.

Go West, Not-So-Young Man

Audubon had always wanted to travel across the American frontier, but his schedule did not permit it until 1843. At the age of 58, accompanied by friends and assistants, he embarked on this trip full of excitement, constantly noting in his journals the exuberant diversity of the landscape and the animal life, the military forts he visited, the pioneer settlements, and the miscellaneous groups of trappers and Indians he came across. Game was plentiful, and he and his party shot numerous animals for sport, to preserve as specimens, and, as usual, for food.

During this journey through the American West, he was struck by the slaughter of the bison herds and commented in his journal: "What a terrible destruction of life as it were for nothing or next to it, the flesh left to rot. The prairies are literally covered with the skulls of the victims. This cannot last. Even before many years, the buffalo will have disappeared."

Although the primary purpose for the eight-month trip was scientific, Audubon was not successful in discovering many new species of quadrupeds. But he did identify 14 new species of birds, which were incorporated into later octavo editions of *The Birds of America*. Overall, however, the group was more preoccupied with buffalo-hunting than with drawing or collecting specimens. To Bachman's disappointment, the expedition resulted in little artistic output, but provided good copy for the newspapers.

The Frontier

Western life and scenery became the subject of a number of American artists, but their goals were different from Audubon's. The Swiss-born **Karl Bodmer** (1809–1893) accompanied the German Prince Maximilian of Wied-Neuwied on a scientific expedition up the Missouri River from 1833 to 1834 and portrayed the Indians and landscape of the Great Plains in precisely drawn watercolors and oils, such as *Indians Hunting the Bison* (1833–34). Among those working contemporaneously with Audubon were **Charles Deas** (1819–1867), a painter of romantic and dramatic western scenes such as *Long Jakes, the Rocky Mountain Man* (1844); **Alfred Jacob Miller** (1810–1874), who recorded Indian life in watercolors and oils like *Hunting the Grizzly Bear* (c. 1839); and **John Mix Stanley** (1814–1872), who also painted western scenes such as *Buffalo Hunt on the Southwestern Prairie* (1845). **George Catlin** (1796–1872) spent six years, beginning in 1832, depicting Indian life and exhibiting works like *Buffalo Chase, Mouth of Yellowstone* (1832) in his Indian Galleries in North America and Europe.

TOP
Shipping box for John James Audubon's prints.

ABOVE
John James Audubon's beaded purse, made by his wife, Lucy, and used from 1826 to 1828 during his visit to England

Barred Owl
c. 1821
Watercolor
pastel
graphite
and ink
on paper
37 ½ x 25 ⅜"
(95.3 x 64.5 cm)

From Feathers to Fur

Audubon's method and style of painting remained the same for *The Quadrupeds* as it had been for *The Birds of America*, even to the extent of direct copying. The eastern gray squirrel portrayed in the print of the *Barred Owl* was incorporated into Audubon's later picture of these squirrels for *The Quadrupeds.*

Audubon painted deer, antelope, mice, skunks, lynx, raccoons, porcupines, rabbits, buffalo, bears, rats, and other warm-blooded creatures. Mammals also appeared in some of the oil paintings Audubon produced as gifts or for quick sale for ready cash. There are multiple copies of the *Entrapped Otter* (c. 1827), although his technique in oil never approached the brilliance of his watercolors.

In examining the watercolor of the *Woodchuck* (1841), one finds that the artist lightly sketched the subject and followed the outline closely, a technique similar to the one he used for the birds. Minor changes are visible, but for the most part the first vision remained intact. His ability to depict textures is transferred from feathers to skin and fur. Each hair seems to be painted separately, so finely delineated they appear to be executed with a pen point rather than a pointed brush—but no sign of ink has been found.

In *The Quadrupeds*, Audubon's watercolors were enhanced by small dashes of other mediums, with the same bold design and power of animation in his animals that captivated admirers of *The Birds of America*. Most often, he left the backgrounds for Victor or John to complete, and many of them are quite beautifully executed in prints such as *American Mink, Eastern Gray Squirrel, Eastern White-Footed Mouse, Deer Mouse,* and *Wood Mouse.*

Sound Byte:
"No one, I think, paints in my method; I, who have never studied but by piece-meal, form my pictures according to my ways of study. For instance, I am working on a Fox; I take one neatly killed, put him up with wires and when satisfied with the truth of the position, I take my palette and work as rapidly as possible."

—JOHN JAMES AUDUBON, January 1827

Va-Va-Viviparous!

The Viviparous Quadrupeds of North America, containing 150 hand-colored lithographs of mammals, was published between 1845 and 1848 in its imperial folio size, produced in three volumes by the lithographer John T. Bowen in Philadelphia and issued at intervals. There were about 300 subscribers, some of whom Audubon had procured before his death. The accompanying text was written by Bachman and Victor

Woodchuck
1841
Watercolor and
pencil on paper
23 x 33 $^{11}/_{16}$"
(51.75 x 75.94 cm)

*Eastern Gray
Squirrel*
1849
Lithograph
27 ½ x 23"
(61.88 x
51.75 cm)

SCIURUS CAROLINENSIS .GMELIN.
CAROLINA GREY SQUIRREL.

American Museum of Natural History, New York

Audubon using John James Audubon's journals, and it was published additionally in three separate octavo volumes—1846, 1851, and 1854 (six additional pictures were added by John Woodhouse Audubon for the 1854 version). This miniature version dropped the word *viviparous* (which means "to produce young live from the body") in its second edition and sold around 2,000 copies.

Differences in popularity between *The Birds* and *The Quadrupeds* may be due to the fact that Audubon painted only about half of the mammals. The others were created by John Woodhouse Audubon, with a very few made after his father's death—and the latter lack his father's dynamic hand. The fact that many of the animals were drawn from specimens rather than from real life may also account for their relative lack of animation. Yet the series remains a remarkable *tour de force* in the tradition of the great master John James Audubon and deserves reexamination as a work of art as well as a scientific document.

Death of a Master

In the 1840s, after years of hard work and just as he was beginning to enjoy the fruits of his labor, Audubon began to suffer mental deterioration, possibly Alzheimer's disease. His last years were spent at Minnie's Land in mental oblivion, and he died in 1851 at the age of 65. His sons, who had built homes for themselves and their families on the property, died less than ten years later, leaving Lucy Audubon to support the extended family all on her own. Fate was unkind to Lucy. After years of struggle, she now faced a quick succession of deaths in her family. Like many a pioneer woman, she had withstood endless hardships and had assisted her husband in far more than household chores: She wrote letters for him, copied manuscripts, helped to market his work, and perhaps even drew a bird or two.

The family deaths compelled her to rent out her house on Minnie's Land and move in with Victor's remaining family. Destitute, she put Audubon's original watercolors up for sale in November 1861. Initially no one was interested, since the Civil War had begun and there was little ready cash available. She offered the watercolors to several institutions, but only the British Museum showed even a minor interest.

The Almighty Lucy

Like her husband, Lucy eventually proved to be a forceful saleswoman. In 1862, she presented the work before a committee at The New-York Historical Society. Hour after hour, she turned the large pages, quietly explaining to the men on the committee the circumstances under which each was painted and the hardships

Lucy Audubon

Sharp-Shinned Hawk
1836-37

Audubon had endured. She had to coax the society into buying all that she could sell, later offering them the *Ornithological Biography* for as little as a dollar a volume. The committee arranged to raise the purchase money by subscription and sent a circular to potential subscribers urging: "As a work of our national art and our natural history, this opportunity should not be lost, to deposit near the home of the distinguished artist, these memorials of his genius, according to his wish, in a secure place like that of the Art Gallery of this Incorporation."

The New-York Historical Society to the Rescue

Fortunately, The New-York Historical Society raised the $4,000 necessary for the purchase of this national treasure (a sum one writer likened to the paltry $24 paid to the Indians for the island of Manhattan). Today, some individual Audubon bird prints sell for more than $100,000. Complete sets sell for $3,000,000 to $4,000,000 each. Owing to her strength and prescience, Lucy Audubon had managed to preserve the incredible original watercolors for *The Birds of America* by a remarkable American artist.

When Lucy tried to sell the engraved copper plates ten years later, she met with even greater resistance. Several had been destroyed or damaged previously, and in 1871 the bulk of the remainder were sold for the value of the metal and melted down. Only about 78 remain, saved for posterity by a young man whose father was the manager of the smelting firm that bought the plates.

The Audubon Society

The invincible Lucy Bakewell Audubon lived until 1874. She published a biography of her husband and opened a private school out of her second-floor bedroom at age 70 in order to support her grandchildren. One of her pupils was a boy named **George Bird Grinnell**, whose family had moved to the area near Audubon's estate, Minnie's Land, in 1857. More than his daily lessons, what left a lasting impression on the young Grinnell were the artifacts in the house belonging to the late artist-naturalist. Among the mounted animal and bird skins was a large portrait of Audubon dressed in buckskin, holding his gun, along with copies of his *Ornithological Biography*.

In 1886, Grinnell—then editor of *Forest and Stream* magazine—encouraged readers to join him in forming the first bird-preservation organization to help stop the relentless slaughter of birds. He named it **The Audubon Society** in honor of the artist whose pictures he had loved as a boy. Thousands of people immediately joined the society, more than Grinnell had anticipated, and his effort was aborted by 1888. Audubon societies were subsequently established independently in a number of states. In 1901, some of the societies formed a loose alliance, and by 1905 they incorporated into the National Association of Audubon Societies for the Protection of Wild Birds and Animals.

The Audubon Society is responsible for having helped protect wild animals throughout the world by lobbying for stronger international laws. The society has also inspired the creation of environmental groups everywhere.

Sound Byte:
"It is somewhat singular that my enthusiastic husband stuggled to have his talents published in his Country and could not; and I have struggled to sell his forty year's labor and cannot."
—LUCY AUDUBON, 1863, in a letter to The New-York Historical Society

A Lasting Contribution

Although his style of painting and interest in natural history are wholly consistent with the time in which he lived, John James Audubon's dedication and persistence in completing *The Birds of America* and his initiation of a rather extraordinary project, *The Viviparous Quadrupeds of North America*, make him an outstanding figure in the tradition of series publications on natural history. His work has endured because of his unique artistic ability, his outstanding compositional sensibility, and his technical virtuosity. No matter how trivialized Audubon's work has become by commercial reproductions, it retains its appeal. That is the endurance of great art.

OPPOSITE
Detail from
Carolina Parakeets
1825

John James Audubon
c. 1835
Engraving

Notwithstanding his scientific contributions, his identification of new species, and his ultimate acceptance into numerous scientific societies, Audubon's most significant achievement is that of his extraordinary art. He struggled during his lifetime to make ends meet and to promote his life's work, and probably would revel in the fact that a complete set of *The Birds of America* today sells for millions of dollars. He has become an American national treasure, a universally recognized symbol to the world of America's twin ambitions in art and in science.